Franco Migliorini

Luigi Latini

Gardens
from the Air

FRANCES LINCOLN

Original title: *Giardini visti dal cielo*
© 2004 Colophon srl, San Polo 1978, Venezia
Text: Luigi Latini, Franco Migliorini
Photographs: Mauricio Abreu (Tips): 225. Archivio Scala:
14-15. Bertram-Luftbild München-Haar: 104-105,
108-109, 118-119, 120-121, 122-123, 124-125, 126-127,
128-129, 202-203, 204-205, 212-213, 215, 216-217,
218-219, 242-243, 252-253. Yann Arthus-Bertrand
(Altitude): 16-17, 68-69, 76-77, 78-79, 81, 87, 88-89,
90-91, 92-93, 94-95, 102-103, 106-107, 110-111,
112-113, 114-115, 116-117, 142-143, 144-145, 146-147,
148-149, 160-161, 222-223, 228-229, 244-245, 246-247,
248-249, 250-251. Michel Bureau (Altitude): 84-85.
Jason Hawkes 96-97, 98-99, 164-165, 167, 168, 168-169,
170-171, 173, 174-175, 176-177, 179, 180-181, 182-183,
184-185, 186-187, 188-189, 190-191, 192-193, 194-195,
196, 196-197, 198-199, 200-201, 210-211, 221.
Heinz Hebesein (Iberimage): 18-19, 22-23.
Helen Hiscocks (Altitude): 74-75, 82-83, 162-163.
R. van der Meeren (Altitude): 158-159. Daniel Philippe
(Altitude): 130-131. Donata Pizzi (Tips): 24-25. Pubbli Aer
Foto: 66-67, 100-101, 138-139, 140-141. Miguel Raurich
(Iberimage): 20-21, 226-227, 234-235. Guido Alberto
Rossi (Tips): 26-27, 29, 30-31, 32-33, 34-35, 36-37,
38-39, 41, 42-43, 44-45, 46-47, 48-49, 50-51, 52-53,
54-55, 56-57, 58-59, 60-61, 62-63, 64-65, 70-71, 73,
133, 134-135, 136-137, 150-151, 153, 155, 206-207,
208-209, 231, 233, 236-237, 238-239, 240-241.
Lucien Roulland (Altitude): 156-157.

Gardens from the Air first published in the English language
by Frances Lincoln Ltd, 4 Torriano Mews, Torriano
Avenue, London NW5 2RZ
www.franceslincoln.com
Translation by Caroline Beamish
copyright © Frances Lincoln Ltd 2004

British Library Cataloguing in Publication data
A catalogue record for this book is available from
the British Library

ISBN 0-7112-2448-X

Printed in Italy by Editoriale Lloyd, Trieste

9 8 7 6 5 4 3 2 1

Contents

Introduction 6

The Mediterranean 15
Agdal, Marrakech 16
Alhambra, Granada 18
Generalife, Granada 20
Alcázar de los Reyes Cristianos,
Cordoba 22

A Human Scale:
Gardens in Sixteenth and
Seventeenth Century Italy 25
La Petraia, Castello 26
Boboli, Florence 28
Villa Giulia, Rome 30
Villa d'Este, Tivoli 32
Palazzo Farnese, Caprarola 34
Villa Lante Bagnaia 36
Villa Aldobrandini, Frascati 38
Villa Doria Pamphilj, Rome 40
Giardini del Quirinale, Rome 42
Villa Giusti, Verona 44
Botanic Gardens, Padua 46
Prato della Valle, Padua 48
Villa Emo, Fanzolo 50
Villa Barbaro, Maser 52
Villa Barbarigo, Valsanzibio 54
Villa Manin, Passariano 58
Villa Garzoni, Collodi 60
Villa Torrigiani, Capannori 62
Isola Bella, Lake Maggiore 64
Villa Carlotta, Lake Como 66

The Enlightenment Garden 69
Chenonceaux 70
Fontainebleau 74
Luxembourg Gardens, Paris 76
Tuileries, Paris 78
Vaux-le-Vicomte 80
Chantilly 84
Park of Saint-Cloud 86
Versailles 88

Courances 94
Hampton Court 96
La Granja de San Ildefonso 100

In the Image of Versailles,
Courtly Gardens in Eighteenth
Century Europe 103
Nymphenburg 104
Schleissheim 106
Augustusburg, Brühl 108
Herrenhausen, Hannover 110
Charlottenburg 114
Sanssouci, Potsdam 116
Schwetzingen, Baden-Württemberg 118
Schlossgarten, Karlsruhe 120
Eremitage Garten, Bayreuth 122
Sanspareil, Bayreuth 124
Hofgarten, Veitshöchheim 126
Wilhelmshöhe, Kassel 128
Peterhof (Petrodvorets),
St Petersburg 130
Reggia, Caserta 132
Villa Pisani, Stra 134
Stupinigi, Turin 136
Racconigi, Turin 138
Villa Reale, Monza 140

From Fortress to Garden 143
Kronborg, Helsingør 144
Fredensborg 146
Muider, Muiden 150
Albi 152
Angers 154
Hautefort 156
Roche Courbon, Saint Porchaire 158
Villandry 160

The Reconquest of Nature 165
Ickworth House 166
Longleat House 168
Blenheim Palace 170
Hatfield House 172
Wilton House 174

Bowood House 176
Castle Howard 178
Charlecote 180
Chatsworth House 182
Cliveden 186
Floors Castle 188
Buckingham Palace, London 190
Kew Gardens, London 192
Waddesdon Manor 194
Dunrobin Castle 196
Hever Castle 198
Worlitz, Dessau 202
Ilm Park, Weimar 204

The Garden in the City 207
St Stephen's Green, Dublin 208
Regent's Park, London 210
Tiergarten, Berlin 212
Schiller Park, Berlin 214
Ohlsdorf Cemetery, Hamburg 216
Volkspark Rehberge, Berlin 218
Sissinghurst 220
Monet's Garden, Giverny 222
Monserrate, Sintra 224

The Contemporary Garden 227
Linderhof 228
Miramare, Trieste 230
Villa Taranto, Pallanza 232
Parque Guëll, Barcelona 234
La Gamberaia, Settignano 236
La Foce, Chianciano 238
Parco Sigurtà, Valeggio 240
Olympia Park, Munich 242
La Villette, Paris 244
Parc André Citroën, Paris 246
Parc Bercy, Paris 248
La Défense, Paris 250
Hotel Kempinski, Munich 252

Bibliography 254
Index 255

Introduction

The Origin of the Garden

Whether by chance or by design, we have all at some time found ourselves in the open air gazing at a natural view (or a view that we assume to be natural), and experienced its power to stir our innermost feelings and arouse unexpected emotions. These feelings and emotions are sometimes so strong that they can produce an extraordinary sense of expectation: we expect the beauty which is revealed before our eyes, we expect this perfect correspondence between the external and the internal, imagination and reality, the world and ourselves. These are feelings that have been experienced by man throughout the ages: joy, serenity, fulfilment. Here is the material manifestation of a superior world which exists, yet has to be discovered and conquered if we want to make it our own.

Magic, divine expression, profound spirituality, life force, creative inspiration – all these have been invoked in an attempt to explain the existence of a "spirit of place", that elusive presence, found only in certain (very few) locations. The elusiveness of the spirit of place helps to explain why man has tried to emulate and reproduce these natural manifestations, reorganising the natural landscape according to a set of symbols, allegorical references and aesthetic codes. As in the case of a temple or a tomb, the process of reorganisation is guided by spiritual needs. Compared with these, however, the process seems strongly imbued with physical vitality and sensory gratification: an expression of optimism and a very positive view of self and of the world. The search for beauty has become an expression of human emancipation. This is the road down which we have to go to locate the birthplace of the garden. The evocative power of beauty, is the distinguishing feature of this unique means of expressing human creativity, over all the centuries in which organised society has developed – historically, artistically and culturally.

The garden, with its memories of the lost gardens of the past, is a constant feature of civilian life, a message from centuries gone by which never loses the ability to communicate man's yearning for aesthetic experience. Freed from the exigencies of everyday life, the garden aims to create a state of well-being which transcends materialistic preoccupations. It represents an attempt to open oneself to eternity, to project one's being towards the infinite, to embed the physical semblances of which it consists in one particular place. The garden prefigures the idea of the earthly paradise. Simple, ephemeral elements – earth, water, plants, flowers and ornaments – combine to create images of beauty and eternal bliss, mapping the way forward to ourselves and to our successors.

Nature, the primordial life force, is the ultimate garden designer; we attribute to the garden the spiritual role of the mother of all living things. When combined together in ways designed to suggest the power of repro-

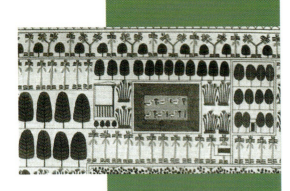

duction and the miracle of creation, the products of the garden – water, trees, flowers, fruit – transcend their normal utilitarian significance, becoming symbols or omens. We are encouraged to look beyond basic needs towards the ultimate essence.

From the earliest times, the evolution of the garden has been the result of the combination of formal and figurative solutions based on the use of geometry (as the matrix for spatial construction), botany (or developing agriculture) and artistic symbolism (to provide meaning which transcends the objects represented).

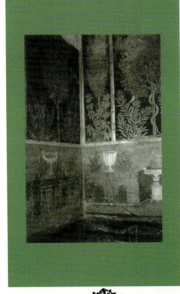

We are all familiar with the iconography of the modern European or American garden. Embedded within it we find references, typologies, figurative and allegorical patterns rooted in distant tradition. The tradition goes back to the civilisations of Mesopotamia and Persia; it was then filtered through ancient Egypt, was consolidated in Greek civilisation, diffused throughout the Roman Empire, was present during the lengthy Arab expansion, then became deeply rooted in mediaeval thought and practice. It was later reinterpreted during the Renaissance and thus influenced the development of the modern garden.

There are certain words and images which can assist us in our quest for this often unconscious reference to the historical continuity that is embodied in the idea of a garden. The Persian *pairidaeza*, preserved in the stylised patterns of the Persian carpet, became the *pardes* of the Old Testament, and the *paradeisos* of the Greeks. All these words convey the idea of the absolute implicit in the notion of the garden. The *peristylon* (colonnade), *peripteros* (pergola) and *peripaton* (promenade) embody some of the constructional principles of Greek garden design, used at a later date around the shores of the Mediterranean. The Roman *hortus conclusus* refers to the garden, particularly the kitchen garden, surrounded by an enclosing fence or hedge. This formal and conceptual idea of the garden was preserved in the mediaeval *hortus gardinum* within the monastic *claustrum*. Thus the term *gardinum* (from "gart": to watch, preserve, circumscribe) became current in all European languages (*jardin, garden, Garten*), consolidating the correspondence between the word and its current meaning.

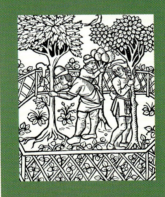

Fresco depicting a garden found in a tomb in Thebes, Egypt, 1405-1370 BC

Floral cubicle, Casa del Frutteto, Pompei, 1ˢᵗ century AD.

The mediaeval garden, from Pietro De Crescenzi, De Ruralium Commodorum, Florence 1495.

Work in the garden, from Pietro De Crescenzi, De Ruralium Commodorum, Florence, 1495.

From the Renaissance onwards, in fact, the definition of the garden became confused with the idea of "park", a word originating from the word *parra* or *barra* – which then became *parricus, parch, barco* and *parco* – meaning a vast enclosed area, usually wooded, and used for hunting and raising cattle. The park carried overtones of power and land ownership, and was for years the prerogative of the aristocracy and ruling houses. During the "modern" period, wooded parks have suffered progressive inroads, both as far as the woodland is concerned and the sporting activities they support. The latter were at first the prerogative of the élite, but are increasingly practiced by the general public. This change signals the entry of the park into contemporary urban civilisation.

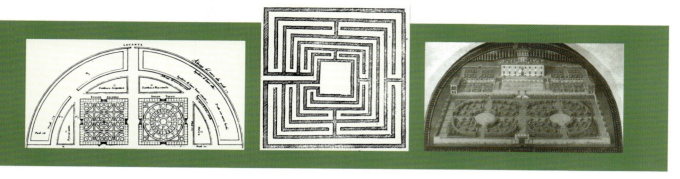

The Botanic Garden, Padua, 1545

Labyrinth, from Sebastiano Serlio, Trattato di architettura, Libro quarto, *Venice 1537.*

Giusto Utens, Villa La Petraia, *sixteenth century.*

From the seventeenth century onwards, large country estates began to be transformed by landscape designers. The explicit intention was to extend new principles of composition to the whole area, to create a single unit. The formal garden was either abandoned or inccorporated. Whatever landscape already existed formed the basis of the new design and was not radically altered.

The Nature of the Garden and the Garden in Nature

The garden was born as a portion of the natural environment adapted to the needs of man, and designed for his physical and spiritual well being. The garden was inspired by nature, but the garden also interpreted and reproduced nature. This is the key to garden reform which began in Renaissance Italy; it was carried out at a time when economic progress released extraordinary wealth and energy into the fields of science, technology and all the arts. This led to a widespread reassessment of the relationship between man and nature in a society busy reorganising itself. Man left the cities and took over the entire territory. The countryside was no longer seen as a *selva oscura* ("a dark wood"), it had become *ager* ("productive land") to be tilled by human hand. As part of this economic, organisational and symbolic transition, the garden became one of the most sophisticated and self-conscious expression of creativity.

Cultivated fields once again became the dominant feature of the landscape. This was due to new ploughing techniques, land reclamation and irrigation, and the sowing, harvesting and commercialisation of agricultural produce. Reclaiming the land was a long process, and extended much further into the countryside than the agricultural areas occupied during the Roman period. The plains were cultivated and so were many hilly areas. New buildings, rustic to begin with and then more aristocratic, began to impart to the features of the landscape that notion of rural labour that is synonymous with the "good management" of the land; in Siena this notion is clearly conveyed through the painted panels of Ambrogio Lorenzetti representing the wealth and produce resulting from good husbandry and good government. The garden, the outward manifestation of economic surplus, thus became a visual and symbolic link between the new aristocratic residence, in town or country, and the land around it. The idea was to domesticate nature, and to extend the philosophical and aesthetic vision of the prevailing sensibility, most clearly manifested in the ceremonial architecture of the Renaissance, to the outside world. At the same time, the countryside was allowed to penetrate the enclosure of the aristocratic residence, thanks to the inclusion of the garden in the architectural design of the whole site. As early as the fifteenth century Leon Battista Alberti in his architectural treatises gives precise details of the terracing to be built

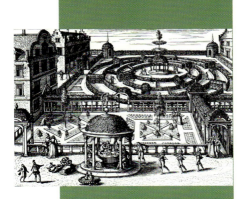

outside the house, laying down strict rules to govern the relationship between garden and landscape. One must complement the other. They should be joined in a fruitful and indissoluble partnership, by the artistic skill of the architect, who will interpret the character of the site and to fix its appearance for ever, using the new criterion of space as a continuum.

Outline History of the European Garden

The history of the garden is the history of an artistic genre in the truest sense. It proceeds hand in hand with (but independently of) the other arts – architecture, painting, sculpture and even literature. Like them, it aims to register and transmit contemporary sensibility. The garden takes its cue from the other arts, accessing the heritage of form, materials and ideas but also revealing its own specific attributes: the garden synthesises all the other arts by constructing outdoor space; it makes landscape a creative endeavour, affected by the hand of man at the highest level.

The Renaissance experience spread throughout all the regions of Italy and Europe, adapting itself to different contexts in which climate and landscape dictated the work of the garden, confirming the symbiotic relationship between the garden and the countryside. As the new nation states gradually formed, from the sixteenth century onwards, Spain, France, England and the other countries of Europe began to influence the development of the garden. The adjustment and alteration of outside space carried strong symbolic overtones.

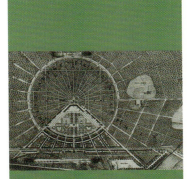

The meaning of the relationship between man and nature, which the Renaissance garden helped to spread throughout Europe, often tended later to become a representation of the relationship between the ruling power and society. The French garden helped to establish this and to promote it. The predominantly flat or lightly undulating countryside around Paris was the scene of new horticultural activity in the seventeenth century. The vision of space which had inspired the Italian garden was dispensed with, and the vast axial perspective, disappearing from sight, multiplied correspondingly. The central fulcrum, represented by the monarch's palace, dominated this perspective, signifying the sovereign's power over the whole of society. The Palace of Versailles, the most grandiose of all, became the model for European courts for more than a century. The continent was dotted with copies and interpretations, built to proclaim the newly acquired power of kings or princes by their opulence and majesty. The profile of the states of Europe was being redesigned, and the rulers were keen to impress their presence on the land as a lasting physical testimony to their material strength. A reaction to all this originated in England where, during the course of the eighteenth century, such grandiose and oppressive

Engraving from Hans Vredeman de Vries, Hortorum Viridariorumque Elegantes et Multiplicis formae…, Antwerp, 1583.

André Le Nôtre, Versailles, 1662.

The Tuileries Gardens, from Jacques-Androuet du Cerceau, Les plus excellents bâtiments de France, 1576-79.

Planimetry of Karlsruhe and the Hardtwald, Germany 1715.

Baroque designs were opposed with great determination and lucidity. In reality, alongside the emergence of a new social class, the bourgeoisie, a new aesthetic and social sensitivity was developing outside (and even within) the courts. Behind this new class was hidden a new vision of the relationship between man and nature, no longer viewed through the rigid juxtaposition of geometrical schemes but based on greater respect for unadorned nature. The reaction against the oppressive demands of the axial design – summed up by the abolition of the straight line from garden planning – perhaps symbolises the modern desire for individual liberty which stemmed from reaction to the power of absolute monarchy – a desire symbolised also in scientific and other aesthetic developments.

The English garden represents genuine revolution. It was substantially invented during the last few decades of the seventeenth and the first few of the eighteenth centuries by a group of young landscape designers inspired by a romantic view of nature. This naturalism was fed by the current scientific climate, which encouraged botanical research and experiment. New, exotic species were located and imported, and were then acclimatised in the new glasshouses of the botanical gardens of England. The excitement soon spread to the continent. The reforming zeal continued as industrial expansion got under way, ensuring that green spaces where the labouring classes could spend their leisure time were included in the developing towns. The new city parks carried a hidden message as well, the message of hygiene and emancipation; in the new industrial world, the worship of nature was now part and parcel of the aspiration and expectation of modern man.

With the advent of urban, industrialised society in the nineteenth and twentieth centuries, the garden's most innovative developments were to be made in towns. From being a place set apart, to be used by the élite, the garden became a more declaredly social and urban location, open to all, enriched by new experiments, with new protagonists and new users. From being a place of passive aesthetic contemplation, the garden became a place where leisure time could be enjoyed, by the individual and by society as a whole. Aesthetics and function had to merge and to adopt new practices and ideas. No single aesthetic is dominant today. The classical repertory has been reinterpreted, preserving what it can of its educational impact; today, research and innovation focus substantially on the creative use of technology.

The Experience of the Garden Today

A grand survey of the garden today would reveal first and foremost its universality. The establishment of an appropriate relationship between society and the natural world is shown in our ever expanding cities to be the

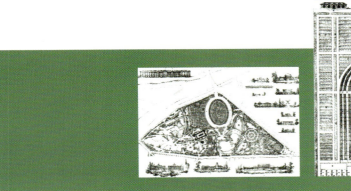

Plan for the enlargement of the Jardin des Plantes in Paris, and for the Jardin pour la naturalisation, by Gabriel Thouin, Plans raisonnés de toutes les espèces de jardins, *Paris 1820.*

Illustration by John C. Loudon, A Treatise on Forming, Improving and Managing Country Residences, *London 1851.*

greatest aspiration of contemporary mass civilisation. The garden continues to fulfil a need and a desire. The spatial constraints of the garden contain the seeds of its continued popularity, the metaphor for a common aspiration: to exceed the limits of the material world by using all that the material world has to offer.

The garden is at once art and science, locus and symbol, concreteness and abstraction. As a manifestation of a possible synthesis, the garden absorbs many diverse disciplines – as they present themselves. Soil and hydraulic engineering, agronomy and botany, technology and art, architecture and town planning. From time to time the garden absorbs what precedes it and what follows it. Recently this combination of practical and theoretical subjects has been defined as "landscape architecture", a term intended to cover everything, from the original art of "topiary" to the construction of parks in the landscape; and more recently to urban parks and, more generally, to contemporary open spaces. In addition, the garden is a living environment: like all living things it is born, grows, declines and dies. This is the condition that binds together the history of all the gardens that ever existed. Its inherent, often sophisticated artificiality is at once a strength and a weakness. The garden is tended according to daily, seasonal, and annual rhythms, by expert staff, dedicated full time to the care of the precarious equilibrium of every single garden.

Because it is an open space, the garden is subject to all climatic influences; because it is an artificial environment it requires continual assistance; because it is a scenic and symbolic space it is subject to fluctuations of taste, and to the constraints of the message it is designed to convey. When one of these conditions changes, then the garden also changes, either by the hand of nature or of man, or of both. The passage of time therefore has a strong bearing on the garden. The oldest gardens to be seen today are partial or complete copies of the original versions, copied more or less faithfully; apart from any other considerations, this is because the original plant species have been replaced thanks to developments in botany or, more frequently, thanks to gradual changes in taste and technology. Gardens with a lot of architectural and stone features survive better, provided that man respects their integrity. Some very long-lived species of trees survive, but plants and shrubs do not. War, famine, drought, epidemics, economic recessions bring changes to gardens, sometimes changing them completely. This is sometimes followed by refurbishment and new splendour, sometimes by abandonment and eventual disappearance.

Garden restoration today is the subject of academic research, and also of empirical procedure. Its adherents follow various philosophical tendencies which relate to the philosophy of restoration and conservation in general. The garden is to be seen as the product of deliberate human intervention in a given historical and spatial

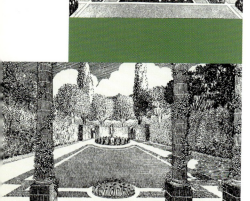

Flower Garden, Hoole House, in The Gardener's Magazine, London 1826.

Project for Leclerc and Rabussier from Jean Claude Nicholas Forestier, Jardins: Carnet de plans et de dessins, *Paris 1920.*

Plan for a garden on a rectangular site by Jean Claude Nicholas Forestier, Jardins: Carnet de Plans et de dessins, *Paris 1920.*

context; it has significance from the point of view of civilisation in general and therefore bears a universal message. The garden links towns and villages in a packed historical and geographical landscape, where a civil and artistic substratum binds together things that military and political history has often divided and altered. The development of the European garden has to be measured on a continental scale, as the fruit of space as well as time, and in particular of landscapes which, with the differences they possess, have been able to catch man's sensitivity over the years in various ways, ultimately binding together our common history in a continuous play of innovation, emulation, and restoration. These results have enriched an itinerary which has evolved according to the particular nature of the different regions, from whence the innovations spread over the whole continent.

Any descriptive sequence used, therefore, must be a sequence of examples, described historically and geographically but the country or region always confers a characteristic flavour to the examples it offers. The ineffable atmosphere conveyed to the visitor by each garden is guaranteed. This atmosphere is not created only by forms and colours, it is created by multi-sensory perceptions in every sphere: olfactory, thermal, acoustic, tactile and even psychological. None of this can really be reproduced, and it is better that this should be so: it is better that every garden should provide a different and unique experience, and should leave a sensation transcending visual memory. It might be useful to read the common history of the garden in detail, through examples which, in order to be communicable, require the abstract view provided by the aerial photograph. As with the process of topographical drawing and two-dimensional design accompanying the birth of a garden, the view from above reveals symbolic and territorial connections which the visitor to the garden cannot completely grasp. The search for high places, such as towers, terraces, pagodas or minarets from which to overlook the design, or to get the sense of a place in its entirety, runs right through the history of the garden; today it is enriched by a new tool, the aeroplane. From above the earth's crust the garden has the traits of an ideal topography, which only the view from above allows us to appreciate; the eye can compare the infinite adaptations of the designed surface with the reality offered by nature. This type of image conveys the synthesis of the usual and the unusual in each garden, giving the spectator the sense of a great event, documented and stimulated by the image. Thus stimulated, it is hoped that curiosity will encourage the observer to experience what he has seen directly. But only when he visits the garden in person will he enjoy the sense of complete gratification which is the raison d'être of every garden.

Wall fresco with garden, Museo Nazionale
Romano, Rome, Italy, first century

The Mediterranean

The shores of the Mediterranean have provided the background to a thousand years of garden history, supporting and sustaining the art of gardening in a wide variety of conditions and locations. The prolonged stagnation of mediaeval Europe stands in stark contrast to the burgeoning culture of the Arab world; the Agdal in Marrakesh (twelfth century) is a remarkable illustration of the survival of this culture. This garden provides us with a complete picture of ancient forms of irrigation and cultivation on a vast scale; its very straightforward chequerboard design embodies the tradition and basic principles of the Mediterranean garden: the sensual interpretation of a utilitarian design. We find the same relationship of land to water in a similarly arid region, Andalusia, in the two great gardens in Granada (fifteenth century), the Alhambra and the Generalife, indissolubly linked together in the history of the garden. The gardens are perched on an eminence in the centre of the city, with the great water supply of the Sierra Nevada towering above them. They reflect their mediaeval Arab origins, with the formal garden expanded to match the scale of the Alhambra, the royal palace of the Almohads, and the *huerta*, the vegetable garden in the next door Generalife promoted to royal dignity as a place of repair for the monarchs. The Alhambra garden reproduces the contemplative intimacy of the domestic garden, but with the wealth of ornament and cunning artifice reserved for royal residences; the Generalife garden is more "rustic" in layout, with the planting echoing the architectural model that is its inspiration. The huge scale of the vegetable garden is emphasised by the fact that it is built on a hill.

The same mixture of Mediterranean layout and memories of the Arab world can be found in the gardens of the Alcázar de los Reyes Cristianos in Cordoba (sixteenth century); water still has a vital role to play, collected here in the great central pool which dominates the garden plan. The spatial and figurative design is beginning to reflect the traditions of the Renaissance, Italian and European.

Agdal, Marrakech, Morocco, twelfth century

Alhambra, Granada, Spain, fifteenth century

Generalife, Granada, Spain, fifteenth century

Alcázar de los Reyes Cristianos, Cordoba, Spain,
sixteenth century

Villa Lante, detail, Bagnaia, Italy, sixteenth century

A Human Scale
Gardens in Sixteenth and Seventeenth Century Italy

La Petraia, Castello, Florence, Italy, 1530

During the sixteenth century, Italy developed a thriving and highly distinctive garden culture, within the cities and outside. The Italian gardens of this period can be identified by their structure, materials, use of space and general iconography. Their strongest identifying features, however, are the way the area around buildings is interpreted, and the close links forged by the garden with the surrounding area: cultivated land encircled by woodland, steep hills and well-drained plains, roads and canals all illustrate the new territorial and political topography of the Italian Renaissance. This crucial chapter in the history of the European garden was linked above all to the construction of the "villa gardens" which expressed their owner's desire to escape the *negotium* of the city for the *otium* of the country; our image of the ideal Italian landscape has been indelibly influenced by these gardens.

The roots of this development can be found in Tuscany, where the Medici rulers built a series of residences outside Florence. The papal gardens of Rome were easily the most spectacular manifestations of the new trend, which also spread to the Veneto. In the Veneto, however, the gardens were less ostentatious, although no less original. Before long such gardens came to be built all over Italy, and their characteristics and symbolic message varied widely; what linked them was the skill with which each garden was linked to the architectural features within it, to local climatic and environmental conditions, hydraulic machinery, botanical collections, the passion for the ancient world and artistic invention. The features to be found in such Italian gardens – grottoes, nymphaea, pools and water features, pergolas, mazes and labyrinths, lemon groves and so on, artfully disposed between the residence and the distant landscape - created a completely new topography whilst also symbolically reducing the universe to a human scale.

Near Castello, the villa and garden of La Petraia stand on an eminence, facing south over the plain towards the city of Florence. The large building with its tower turns its back on the wooded slope behind, and is built on the first of three terraces which constituted the original shape of the garden in Medici times. The highest level – the "level of the Figurina" – leads to an intermediate terrace, with a pool and a flower garden, and then to a larger flat area with an orchard (in Medici times), now a formal garden with box hedges and flowers in a broad elliptical enclosure.

At Boboli, within the city walls of Florence, the Medicean garden is one of the most celebrated in the history of European gardening. The Boboli Gardens lie between the bastions of Fort Belvedere above, and the vast mass of Palazzo Pitti, on the edge of the city, and are built along the central axis of Brunelleschi's building. The garden was developed in two distinct phases: in the sixteenth century a garden was created behind the palace; during the succeeding century it was extended up the south-west facing hill, along the great cypress avenue. The Boboli Gardens – acquired by Eleanora, wife of Cosimo I – were designed by Niccolò Pericoli, known as Il Tribolo who, with numerous other artists, managed to transform an abandoned stone quarry into a spectacular amphitheatre surrounded by shrubberies, "mazes" and orchards. Beyond the amphitheatre, the complex architecture of plants and shrubs is enhanced by an imposing perspective; a broad avenue of cypresses leads down the hill flanked by high hedges containing wild areas and mazes, grottoes and waterfalls, until it reaches the Vasca dell' Isola, a dramatic Baroque garden with statues and citrus trees in tubs which closes the perspective.

During the second half of the sixteenth century, Roman interest in the classical world and the particular combination of the Pontine Marshes and the hills of Rome, produced an astonishing crop of large houses and gardens on the hills of Tivoli, Caprarola and Frascati. Just outside the Porta del Popolo, on the Via Flaminia, Villa Giulia was built in such a way as, in the words of Ammanati, to "comply with a beauteous and pleasing valley". In 1550, as soon as he was elected pope, Julius III commissioned three celebrated architects, Bartolommeo Ammanati, Giorgio Vasari and Jacopo Barozzi, known as Il Vignola, to construct him a dwelling in various phases. Within a rectangular site, the villa consists of a sequence of buildings complete with loggias, courtyards and gardens which unfold along the main central axis, facing each other. The central courtyard contains a nymphaeum two storeys high, designed to emphasise the abundance of the water that gushes from it, flowing down to fill the public drinking fountains.

Water was the central feature of every Roman garden design, both for its aesthetic qualities and its symbolic significance. Water was harnessed and channelled with skill and taste into cascades, nymphaea, fountains and water features: its acoustic and sensory qualities were also exploited to their best advantage. Villa Giulia heralds a new phase in the art of the garden. The factors on which it is based were also of critical importance in the construction of the gardens of Villa d'Este in Tivoli.

The appointment by Julius III of Cardinal Ippolito d'Este as governor of Tivoli, was the cue for the ambitious reconstruction of the gardens. The terrain is precipitous, presenting a drop of about forty-five metres from the entrance to the lower level of the gardens. A complex system of pipe work captures the waters of the Aniene and feeds an imposing, theatrical group of fountains, with pools and canals located all over the garden. The water features were designed by Pirro Ligorio to celebrate both the site and the glory of its owner.

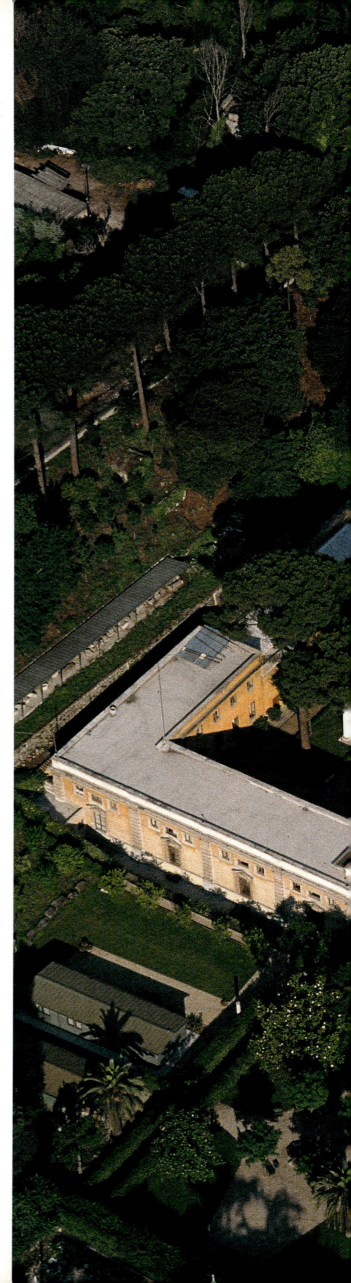

Villa d'Este, Tivoli, Italy, 1560

Villa Manin, Passariano, Italy, seventeenth century

In Tuscany, in the first half of the seventeenth century, the garden of Villa Garzoni at Collodi clearly illustrates Baroque taste; a kind of amphitheatre has been created along the steep side of the hill. Here a series of terraces with espaliered fruit trees, squared at the sides by tall clumps of ilex, descend towards the flat part of the lower garden where there are two large circular pools and a *parterre de broderie*. During the eighteenth century, the garden was enhanced by a watercourse along the slope and a "green theatre", a classic garden accessory frequently to be found around Lucca in the seventeenth and eighteenth centuries.

A majestic avenue of cypresses leads up to Villa Torrigiani in Camigliano, near Capannori. Today, this stands out as the most opulent of all the villas to be found in the countryside around Lucca. In the seventeenth-century garden, the French style is carefully adapted to the forms of the Tuscan landscape. Nicolao Santini, owner of the villa and ambassador of the State of Lucca to the court of Louis XIV, was the creator of this cultural extravagance; today the garden has been returned to its sixteenth-century plan. Survivals of the radical alterations made in the nineteenth century include the pools in front of the house and, most importantly, the series of spaces and baroque architectural details – the fish pond with its statues and bowls of citrus fruits, the steps and the lower "garden of Flora", an elegant area with flower beds and a pavilion-nymphaeon with celebrated fountains at the far end.

Villa Torrigiani, Capannori, Italy,
seventeenth century

No less surprising are the gardens to be found on the banks of the northern lakes, where the imposing backdrop of the Alps and the changing surface of the water accompany and enhance the appearance of every garden. Isola Bella, on Lake Maggiore, was built between 1630 and 1670 at the request of Count Carlo Borromeo. The profile of the entire island was completely altered to resemble a kind of ship; the sides of the ship are closely terraced and furnished with flower beds, ponds, fountains and statues.

In northern Italy the traditional plan of the formal "Italian" garden inevitably merged with the romantic Alpine scenery of the lakes; another example, the Villa Carlotta, was built on Lake Como a century later. Here in 1735 a formal garden was constructed to descend gradually to the shores of the lake via a series of terraces and steps. In the nineteenth century, a large "English" park was created behind the villa to provide a steep and picturesque backdrop.

Isola Bella, Lake Maggiore, Italy, 1630-70

Villa Carlotta, Lake Como, Italy,
eighteenth century

Vaux-le-Vicomte, France,
seventeenth–nineteenth century

The Enlightenment Garden

Chenonceaux, France, sixteenth century

It was not until about the year 1600 that the French garden began to assume an identity of its own. Before that, for more than a century, French gardeners had taken their inspiration from Italy. Olivier de Serres published his first book on agriculture, *Le Théâtre d'agriculture*, in 1600; this is a systematic exposition of the new principles of gardening taken from examples already existing in France, sufficient in number by this time to justify a new theory.

These examples were mainly to be found around Paris, a city surrounded by a vast afforested plateau which allowed gardens in the area to increase in size. The political stability accompanying the reign of Louis XIV, the Sun King, encouraged ambitious design projects which took years to complete. It was in conditions such as these that the extraordinary talent of a garden architect like André Le Nôtre was enabled to flourish over the entire century.

Le Nôtre took over the formal elements of the Italian garden, but organised them around a single visual axis, the *parterre*, which provided the backbone of the whole garden. In addition to this, he paid scientific attention to trees and wooded areas, an essential part of the French garden; water also was always present, acting as a kind of great mirror to reflect the sky and the features of the garden.

The garden surrounding the Château de Chenonceaux is designed in direct relationship to the waters of the river Cher, which bisects the garden in the middle, crossing the axis of the main pathway: a bridge joins the two sides of the great wooded area. The woodland is furrowed by a network of paths which create star shaped crossroads where they meet, and distant views. The gardens commissioned by Diane de Poitiers, to whom the castle was given by Henri II, and that of her rival Catherine de Médicis, are symbolically located on opposite sides of the river. The layout of the second garden is evidently based on the water feature that inspired it, whereas the layout of the garden belonging to Diana, the legitimate owner of the castle, is more durable.

The Château de Fontainebleau was begun in 1528 by François I, who made it his primary residence. The first version of the garden was a joint effort by some of the major Italian architects of the day, for example Serlio and Vignola, who were required to use their building skills in a different context. The garden we see today is largely the result of various attempts at redevelopment by Le Nôtre, beginning in 1645; there is also a new section in the "English" style, created in the late Napoleonic period. Many of the most elaborate parts of the garden (the *parterres*, for instance) are now lost; what remains nevertheless gives an idea of the vast scale of the project, whose main feature was its layout.

The Jardin du Luxembourg is the best-preserved of the old gardens in Paris. It was created in the mid sixteenth century at the request of Marie de Médicis as a place where she could escape from the pomp and ceremony of the royal palace. The designer, Salomon de Brosse, was specifically asked to reproduce the peaceful atmosphere of the Boboli Gardens in Florence, considered by his client to be more intimate and meditative than the normal French garden. In spite of a succession of nineteenth-century enlargements and refurbishments in the landscape style, the original structure remains, with the Medici fountain (1602) in the middle surrounded by flower beds and the original terracing.

Chenonceaux, detail, France, sixteenth century

Fontainebleau, France,
sixteenth–seventeenth century

Luxembourg gardens, Paris, France,
sixteenth century

The Tuileries Gardens, on the west side of the Louvre, are the oldest gardens in Paris. They follow the line of the Champs Elysées and were constructed on the enlarged site of an earlier garden. Their design is Florentine, with quadrilateral *parterres* in the mediaeval style. They were redesigned by Le Nôtre in 1664, when the central axis was developed in what had by now become the established style of the French garden, in the city as well as in *châteaux* in the country. The present appearance of the garden is much altered, as a result of the redesign of the *parterres* during the reconstruction of the entrance to the Louvre in 1989.

Tuileries, Paris, France, seventeenth century

Vaux-le-Vicomte dates from the same period as Versailles, and the gardening talent of Le Nôtre was allied here with the genius of the architect Louis Le Vau and the artist Charles Le Brun. The result is a perfect example of the French garden which obeys all the rules, within a perfectly balanced geometrical plan and elegant composition: the scale is large but not bewilderingly so, the feeling one of complete horizontality, embellished by the elaborate layout of the great *parterre* which provides its basic structure. This garden was too beautiful to escape the envy of Louis XIV; its enterprising owner, Superintendent Fouquet, was guilty of trying to rival his ruler in opulence.

The gardens at Chantilly are the most attractive and harmonious of the many gardens designed by Le Nôtre. All the classic components of the French garden can be found there but they are combined in an unusual design, imposed by the constraints of an irregular site. The direction of the canal is not imposed by the presence of the castle: in fact the castle faces a transverse arm of the canal and is entirely surrounded by water. Thanks to the terracing of the surrounding garden a series of views and unexpected perspectives is provided by the division of the principal axis into two parallel axes, east and west. This asymmetry accounts for the extraordinary beauty of the garden, which constantly surprises the visitor. The plan might be seen as prophetic: if the designer's hand is guided by the nature of the terrain, admirable results can be achieved, results which could never be achieved by any artificial or preconceived plan.

Vaux-le-Vicomte, France,
seventeenth–nineteenth century

Herrenhausen, Hannover, Germany, 1680

Herrenhausen, detail, Hannover, Germany, 1680

Charlottenburg, Germany, eighteenth century

Sanssouci, Potsdam, Germany, 1744

The spectacular garden of the Sanssouci palace in Potsdam has its own vineyard on a hillside in the centre of a collection of gardens and landscaped parks extending over more than two hundred hectares. The most spectacular part of the garden, which was commissioned by Frederick II of Prussia in 1744, is the sequence of six terraces with steps and lines of clipped shrubs, leading up to a pavilion at the top. From the front, the garden appears as a continuous wall, with the windows of the glasshouses on top and parallel vine trellises below; the undulating movement of the vines gives an upward dynamic which is most attractive and unusual.

Schwetzingen, in Baden-Württemberg, was the summer residence of the Palatine court. Although the palace has mediaeval origins, it took its present form in the mid eighteenth century, with the participation of celebrated architects such as Alessandro Galli da Bibiena and Nicolas de Pigage. The design of the garden and its *parterres* was dictated by the complex shape of the building with its circular end, and by the monumental axis running right across the garden, linking it to the city and to the surrounding countryside.

Still in Baden-Württemberg, the Schlossgarten in Karlsruhe, with its star-shaped plan, is by far the most eloquent example of the attempt to fit everything into a single geometrical scheme: garden, residence, countryside and even the city, founded in 1715. From the tower of the hunting pavilion, placed in the centre of the star, 32 avenues lead away towards a circular walk, 444 metres distant, which also forms the boundary of the garden.

Schwetzingen, Baden-Württemberg, Germany, 1750

Schlossgarten, Karlsruhe, Germany,
eighteenth century

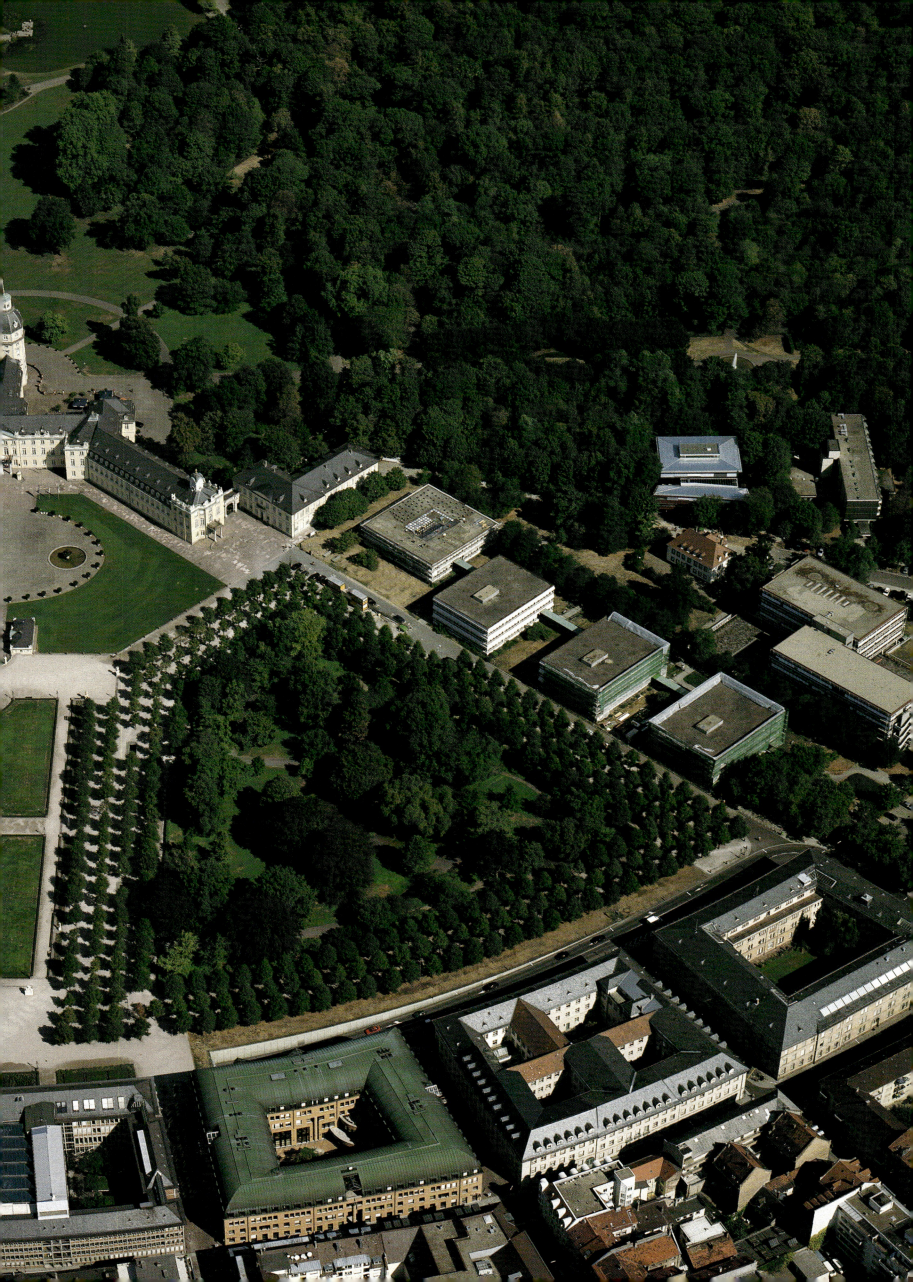

The list of gardens built in Germany in the mid eighteenth century also contains many monumental projects in which the French taste for a formal, unified plan is replaced by a taste for surprise and the unexpected; these designs are more fragmented and contain a mixture of echoes of Italy, references to the exotic and a foretaste of the picturesque. Two Rococo gardens, both in Bayreuth, are worth mentioning in this regard, the Eremitage and Sanspareil. The first was constructed in 1735, when Wilhelmina, the sister of Frederick II, was given the estate which already included a castle and a number of hermitages. The great park of the Eremitage was developed without the benefit of an overall scheme: "gardens" were amalgamated and landscapes linked together. Groves and woodland alternate with grottoes, fountains, water features and flowerbeds, all contrasting very obviously with the surrounding vegetation. The informality of the whole scheme gives a foretaste of the English fashion for landscape design, soon to arrive in Germany.

Eremitage, Bayreuth, Germany, 1735

We owe Sanspareil also to the extravagant taste of the Margravine Wilhelmina, who in this case was keen to transform a wild area – a beech wood dotted with rocky outcrops – into a sequence of moralistic scenes based on a didactic novel by Fénelon, *Télémaque* (1699). The result is a garden which is demonstrably Rococo in style, yet the significance implicit in each section leads us forward to the modern garden of today.

The gardens of Veitshöchheim, the summer residence of the prince-bishop of Würzburg, were begun in 1763 when two existing parks were amalgamated. The result is a garden which is considered the best of all the Rococo gardens in Germany. It contains an elaborate sequence of enclosures and "rooms", corridors, pavilions and mazes, with an extraordinary number of allegorical figures and sculptured groups dotted around it.

Sanspareil, Bayreuth, Germany, eighteenth century

Hofgarten, Veitshöchheim, Germany, 1763

The Wilhelmshöhe park in Kassel presents a grandiose spectacle, inspired by the celebrated Baroque "mechanicals" of Rome, in this case by the "water theatre" in Villa Aldobrandini in Frascati. The garden was conceived, in fact, when the Landgrave returned from a trip to Italy in 1699-1700. The main nucleus of the garden, begun in 1701, was developed on the axis which joins the castle of the prince-electors to the Karlsberg, the mountain dominating the city in the distance. Along this line were constructed a sequence of grottoes, cascades and water features. Above it, the *Wasserschloss*, an octagonal structure, bears the bronze statue of the Farnese Hercules on its central pinnacle; the prospect closes with a waterfall tumbling from a height of at least two hundred metres. At the end of the century, when Wilhelm became prince-elector, the park was named after him and great works were again undertaken. The aim was to create an equally impressive landscaped garden, with an entire ruined castle, an aqueduct and a great cascade.

In Russia the greatest period of garden creation began in the early years of the eighteenth century, when work began on St Petersburg at the initiative of Peter the Great. As in Austria and Germany, the French garden was initially the inspiration, and architects and designers were brought in from France. Peterhof (Petrodvorets), on the Gulf of Finland, is the summer residence of Peter the Great and covers 120 hectares not far from St Petersburg. The garden was designed by J-B Alexandre le Blond, who arrived in Russia in 1716, and was executed later by Niccolò Michetti and the hydraulic engineer Vasily Tuvolkov, who was responsible for the spectacular system of fountains.

130 Peterhof (Petrodvorets), St Petersburg, Russia, 1720

During the eigteenth century, Italy also witnessed some original interpretations of the French model. Of these, the gardens of the Reggia di Caserta, created in the middle of the century, are undoubtedly the most important. Designed by Luigi Vanvitelli, architect of the palace commissioned by Charles III of Bourbon, the gardens cover an exceptionally long slope which begins more than three kilometres from the palace. A spectacular cascade tumbles down the hillside, bringing water to a system of fishponds, pools decorated with sculptured groups and waterways flowing along the garden's axial path, across grassy lawns, shrubberies and transverse avenues.

In the Veneto, in 1735, Alvise Pisani the Doge of Venice undertook the construction of Villa Pisani at Stra, with the intention of producing a garden with the vistas of a French garden. The garden is located in the centre of a wide plain; the back of the house enjoys a theatrical view of the stables. Around this view, which in the twentieth century became a long pond, the various sections of the garden are linked together by geometry dictated by the long perspective axis and by a variety of focal points.

In Piedmont, the country estates of the Royal House of Savoy demonstrate the changes that had come about in gardening and landscape, combining French with Italian models. Not far from Turin, the hunting lodge of Stupinigi, designed by Filippo Juvarra between 1729 and 1731, forms the focal point at the centre of a vast landscape design. The central rotonda, the diagonal arms, the *cour d'honneur* and the gardens all combine to form an open area; the prospect from the hunting lodge extends "to infinity" along the long straight road between the city and the out of town palace.

Of the Savoy residences, the great park of the Castello di Racconigi has undergone more radical transformations than any other. First laid out in the seventeenth century, the gardens gained added lustre in 1670 when they were remodelled to a scheme sent from France by Le Nôtre. A century later, continuing throughout the nineteenth century, the gardens were transformed into a vast romantic park, embellished with neo-Gothic buildings.

One of the earliest examples of an Italian taste for landscape is the park of the Villa Reale di Monza, created at the end of the eighteenth century for Archduke Ferdinand of Austria. This is the most important work commissioned by the Hapsburgs from the architect Giuseppe Piermarini. The park originally covered a small area in front of the villa, with a broad clearing surrounded by thick vegetation, and pastoral scenes with small lakes and winding paths. Today this has been enlarged to cover six hundred hectares.

Villandry, detail, France,
seventeenth–twentieth century

Villandry, France, seventeenth– twentieth century

Landscaped garden, a detail

The Reconquest
of Nature

The growing interest in the natural world in eighteenth-century Europe had its roots in philosophy, science, literature and art, a combination of subjects which found an ideal outlet in gardening. By the reign of Louis XIV the garden already represented the apogee of human ingenuity; the French garden, however, was beginning to be viewed as stiff and pompous, the clear expression of an artificiality which was the reverse of natural.

The first concrete sign of change was the removal of the boundaries separating the garden from the natural world; a ditch, broad and deep enough to isolate the garden without interrupting its continuity with nature was the solution. Gradually but systematically the entire language of the garden began to change, under influence from England. The Chinese garden and the arcadian Mediterranean garden, imbued with nostalgia for the classical world, made their appearance. The straight line vanished and the curved line began to be favoured in all its possible applications, from watercourses to pathways, the edges of copses and islands, and in the form of arched bridges. This tendency was combined with a taste for the neo-classical and the neo-gothic romantic ruin. Large stately homes began to boast a new section designed in the "Anglo-Chinese" style; by the second half of the century the entire layout of the garden had changed.

Most important in bringing about this change was Lancelot Brown, Capability Brown to his contemporaries, who showed exceptional skill in harnessing nature's full potential and revealing the *genius loci* of any landscape. His output over nearly half a century was unrivalled. By this time it was no longer enough to insert a new section in an existing garden: the entire structure had to be renewed. Thus began a period when the gardens of Europe underwent radical transformation. The landscape garden "in the English style" spread over the whole area for at least a century, partly because it could easily be adapted to whatever the local landscape might have to offer. Capability Brown was responsible for the basic composition of the new landscaped garden. First and foremost it had to offer a walk around the whole park, a kind of voyage of discovery; in addition, there had to be woodland surrounding the park, with a large meadow in front of it dotted with isolated clumps of trees and, finally, a natural-looking lake with grassy banks between the house and the landscaped background. The dominant principle was the presence of diagonal views, at an angle to the paths, enjoyed in motion – the exact opposite of the symmetrical and essentially static principle of the French garden.

Ickworth presents a curious marriage between late eighteenth-century architecture, joined to the park by means of a wide rotunda, and the bucolic atmosphere of the vast English park, designed by Capability Brown, in which it is immersed. It boasts miles and miles of paths, a deer park and an ornamental canal which crosses the park. On the south side of the house an Italian garden planted with Mediterranean species reminds visitors of the garden as it originally was.

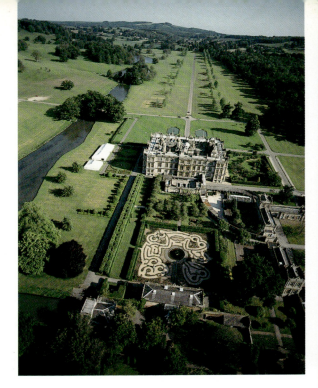

The historic garden at Longleat clearly illustrates the idea of a garden as a succession of events. Capability Brown supervised its first transformation, adding a series of small lakes divided by stands of woodland; this flanks what remains of the central axis in the French style, and the exquisite secret garden with its maze, built in the lee of the house on the west side. On the south side the orangery can be found, and beyond it the arboretum enriched and embellished with exotic species and new landscape effects by designers such as Repton and Russell Page in the nineteenth and twentieth centuries.

A triumphal arch welcomes the visitor to Blenheim, one of the most important examples of English landscape gardening. Here the huge mass of linked buildings, with their courtyards and wings, including the orangery, is accompanied by a series of formal Italian and French gardens, partly rebuilt after their destruction in the eighteenth century, and partly survivals from the late nineteenth century Victorian garden. The broad acres of the park surrounding the great house were landscaped by Capability Brown after 1760 with a lake and cascade. Some of the rectilinear plantings survive from the earlier park, with the original bridge by Vanbrugh linking the two sides of the valley. The eye roams over meadows and clumps of trees, and these eventually merge with the surrounding countryside.

Longleat House, Great Britain, eighteenth–nineteenth century

Blenheim Palace, Great Britain,
eighteenth–nineteenth century

Hatfield, conversely, is an example of the skilful reconstruction of the traditional formal gardens created in the early seventeenth century. Today these surround the building on the east and west sides, whilst the north-south axis is still based on a centralised perspective. The "natural" garden has been recreated around the small original seventeenth-century lake, and the herb and scented gardens have been planted with the same plants that they would have contained between the fifteenth and the seventeenth century. Tens of thousands of bulbs bloom in springtime.

Wilton House, near Salisbury, presents a combination of contrasting features: the eighteenth-century Palladian bridge, a number of ancient monumental oaks in the traditional parkland, and the small scale of the flower, herb and shrub gardens. The visitor's pleasure has been greatly enhanced by the reconstruction and painstaking maintenance of the different gardens, with their neo-classical decorations. A large fountain links the garden with the house, creating an atmosphere of freshness, whilst the espaliered trees, the well-stocked rose garden, the pergola with its climbing varieties, the water garden and the borders with lavender bushes all guarantee a delightful visit.

Bowood House, buried in its enormous park – again the work of Capability Brown – provides a rich mix of classical references: the Doric temple, the cascade, the hermit's cave surrounded by terraces and flower beds in the Italian style, all floating on a perfect carpet of English lawn. New beds of flowering shrubs have replaced the most ornate bedded areas; low hedges outline the geometrical divisions of the spaces around the house, creating a fine balance of scale, form and colour.

Wilton House, Great Britain,
eighteenth–twentieth century

Bowood House, Great Britain,
eighteenth–nineteenth century

Castle Howard is one of the classic examples of the mingling of an original axial design in the French style with the fruits of the English landscape revolution. Of the French garden the central vista survives, with geometrical *parterres* at the front of the building, designed by John Vanbrugh, and a monumental fountain by William A. Nesfield; by contrast, there is an organised wilderness of trees and copses all around, with a huge expanse of water on the other side of the house: here the natural features of the site cannot easily be distinguished from those so skilfully designed to look natural by the landscape architects. The garden today has been enriched with one of the largest rose gardens in the United Kingdom, and an arboretum of substantial scientific value.

Charlecote Park as it appears today is the outcome of vicissitudes of architecture and ownership stretching over eight centuries; the original Tudor red brick can only be seen now in the entrance lodge, but the small park, designed by the omnipresent Capability Brown, still retains its original form and has not been tampered with. A river and a canal border the building on two sides, with a bridge linking the lawns on either side; the house looks across a huge meadow bordered by woodland. From the house, glades and clearings can be seen between the curtain of trees. The house is surrounded by more recent gardens on a much smaller scale, the traditional pleasure gardens for domestic relaxation which can always be found beside a stately home.

Chatsworth is completely different. Four centuries of occupation have left their traces, in spite of a series of alterations and interventions. The most radical intervention was made by Capability Brown, who retained only the cascade and lake of the seventeenth-century design. His "Salisbury meadow", occupying the main axis, is still botanically complete, and it leads the eye towards a distant point on the horizon. In the nineteenth century, Joseph Paxton built the monumental Emperor Fountain and the Great Conservatory (no longer extant). The nineteenth century also saw some perhaps less appropriate decorative and horticultural additions – the arboretum, the pinetum, rhododendrons, the beech avenue and so on. This garden has benefited from recent development, which provides added interest and diversity.

Charlecote Park, Great Britain, eighteenth century.

Chatsworth House, Great Britain,
seventeenth–twentieth century

Chatsworth House, detail, Great Britain,
seventeenth–twentieth century

The house and garden at Cliveden echo the Renaissance atmosphere of the Villa di Frascati in Italy; this effect is mainly achieved by the raising of the house and garden on an artificial embankment, with the garden descending gradually via a succession of terraces. The wholesale removal and installation of an entire balustrade from the Villa Borghese contributes to the illusion. The view from the house thus embraces 360 degrees; the succession of a formal garden, a secret garden and a water garden down the whole length of the property, with the addition of temples, statues and fountains, helps to enhance the classical atmosphere.

The tricky subject of death, and the painful feelings surrounding it, have led cemeteries towards a similar relationship with nature as that suggested by developments in garden landscaping. The vast cemetery at Ohlsdorf, north of Hamburg, presents an interesting illustration of the rules of hygiene governing burial in the late eighteenth century, combined with the idea of the return of the defunct to the welcoming bosom of mother nature. This image is designed to show how life's flow and life's inevitable end can work together to modify the pain of the final withdrawal. After 1877, the landscaping of burial grounds was routinely carried out with extraordinary skill and inspiration.

Volkspark Rehberge, Berlin, Germany,
twentieth century

The Volkspark Rehberge in Berlin is one of the many people's parks created in the 1930s, the outcome of the Movement for Radical Reform's perception that contemporary society as found in German cities was becoming degenerate. The concept of nature as the basis of the German national identity, first met with in the late eighteenth century, crops up again here: the "people's park" is specifically designed for the physical and mental education of the masses. The planting of the park is based strictly on native species, and the landscape design steers well clear of romantic overtones. Elementary geometrical shapes dominate the layout, and any symbolism to be found is generally authoritarian in its intent.

Sissinghurst, by contrast, has become a symbol of contemporary English gardening, thanks to an unique combination of intrinsic beauty and the life story of its creator, Vita Sackville-West, who combined literary talent and horticultural skill to a high degree. This romantic garden extends over four hectares and consists of a series of intimate themed "rooms", richly planted and linked by colour in the manner propounded by Gertrude Jekyll. Unity, variety, inspiration and naturalness: maintaining this delicate and extraordinary achievement, the work of a single outstanding talent, requires total commitment on a daily basis.

Monet's Garden, Giverny, France,
nineteenth–twentieth century

Claude Monet's garden at Giverny, a good example of late nineteenth-century garden design, was both the product and the source of artistic inspiration. The rigour of the plan is mitigated by the impact of shape and colour. Radial views of the garden reveal geometry and monochrome hues; diagonal views, relief and brilliant colour. The garden feels like an outdoor extension of the artist's studio – in which Monet painted one of his best-known series of paintings, *Les Nymphéas*.

The Parco di Monserrate, on the Atlantic coast of Portugal with its damp, temperate climate, is unusual among European gardens for the extraordinary number of botanical species from all over the world it possesses. It was created by an Englishman, James Burt, and conceals a palace in the Arabian style in its midst.

Parque Guell, detail, Barcelona, Spain,
twentieth century

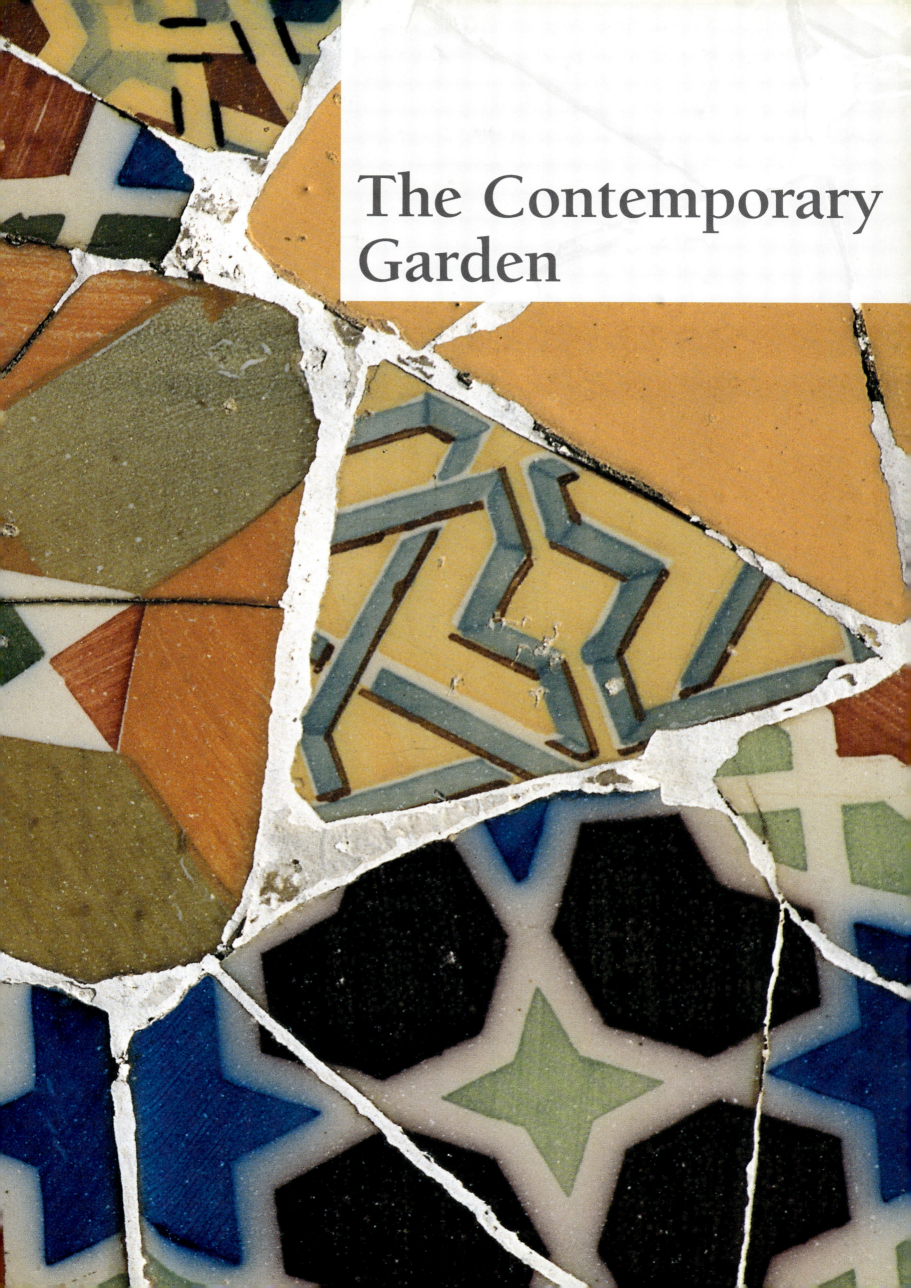

The Contemporary Garden

228   Linderhof, Germany, 1870

The gardens of today evade the classification into fashions and styles that was possible with the gardens of the past. They seem to get lost in a welter of experiments and different circumstances. On the one hand, memories of great examples from the past still linger, on the other the dominance of a single style has long since gone. The result is an aesthetic imbued with tradition which also enjoys great freedom of inspiration. In private gardens this is linked with the aesthetic pleasure of individual well-being; in public gardens the urban open space has to provide the inhabitants of large cities with an opportunity to shake off the constrictions of the city, physically and psychologically. In both cases, private and public, new technology has simplified gardening and made it more popular as a practical activity, rather than simply as a contemplative exercise; in fact, new technology has encouraged the search for a new language of gardening.

The eclecticism that characterised many late nineteenth-century gardens brought to a close a century during which a romantic taste for natural effects prevailed, introducing elements that were forerunners of the "modern" idea of the garden. The park of the castle of Linderhof, the most famous of the fabulous residences of Ludwig II of Bavaria, is an example of the mingling of various styles, with gardens inspired by Italy, France and Germany; there is also a landscaped park peopled with figures from the operas of Richard Wagner.

The castle of Miramare, by the shores of the Gulf of Trieste, is the legacy of one of the grand imperial dynasties of Central Europe. It replicates a late version of the pleasure palaces built on the Italian lakes, in the shadow of the Alps; here instead of the Alps the Adriatic provides the backdrop, with a series of terraces sloping down to the sea.

Villa Taranto in Pallanza is a botanical garden built along the shores of Lake Maggiore. It was commissioned in the 1930s by a Scottish sea captain. The garden of Villa Taranto – like the Hanbury garden in Liguria – perpetuates the Anglo-Saxon dream of a Mediterranean environment providing conditions favourable to the creation of a dramatic and botanically very rich garden.

The Parque Guëll in Barcelona is the product of the extraordinary, unique talent of Antoni Gaudi. Reconciliation between the city and the natural world is achieved through his architecture of the open spaces. The concept as a whole, plus the individual details and colours, aim to create an organic unity. The result is a stimulating and original environment in which nature is interpreted in an imaginative and creative way.

The garden of Villa La Gamberaia in Settignano, near Florence, is a classic example of the interpretation of the Italian tradition by the cosmopolitan visitors who flocked to Italy in the nineteenth and twentieth centuries. In the early 1920s, the owner of the garden, Catherine Jeanne Ghyka, transformed the flat area in front of the villa into a *parterre d'eau*, with box hedges around expanses of water.

The arching evergreens at the far end of the *parterre*, the balustrades and the view of the sunken bowling green all harmonise perfectly with the Florentine hills that surround it.

Ten years later, in the heart of the Sienese hills, the English architect Cecil Pinsent designed the garden of Villa La Foce for Antonio and Iris Origo. The garden is the central nucleus of a much larger project; the couple's aim was to regenerate a large agricultural estate by the use of new technology, along very precise aesthetic lines. In the spirit of the twentieth century, Pinsent designed an impeccable Italian garden: *parterres* and orchards, pools and grottoes encircled by espaliered trees and clumps of cypresses. Long arching pergolas disappear into the landscape of the Val d'Orcia.

The Parco Sigurtà is built on the moraine which closes Lake Garda at its southern tip. It is a curious amateur attempt at modern landscaping, built with the inspiration of an autodidact. The designer has interpreted the atmosphere of the valley of the Mincio by assembling a rich collection of interesting plants, deploying his collection with the taste and inspiration of a genuine landscape artist.

Parque Güell, Barcelona, Spain, twentieth century

La Gamberaia, Settignano, Italy, 1910

La Foce, Chianciano, Italy, 1930

Parco Sigurtà, Valeggio sul Mincio, Italy,
nineteenth century

Olympia Park, Munich, Germany, 1972